Thank you to these knowledge keepers and experts whose contributions helped guide this book toward its goal: to help humanity reestablish a balanced relationship with fire.

BEN CUNNINGHAM-SUMMERFIELD, National Park Service Interpreter, Mountain Maidu/Chippewa
EMILY DAYHOFF, National Park Service Interpreter, Southern Sierra Miwuk
CORY GOEHRING, naturalist
LINNEA J. HARDLUND, giant sequoia forest fellow, fire ecologist, and former wildland firefighter
STEPHEN PYNE, fire historian and professor emeritus, Arizona State University
ANASTASIA ROY, National Park Service
DEAN TONENNA, botanist, Mono Lake Kootzaduka'a

—J. C.

FIRE
SHAPES
THE
WORLD

Joanna Cooke

Illustrated by Cornelia Li & Diāna Renžina

Deep in the wilderness, a fire smolders. It creeps in yellow and crimson bursts, flaring as the wind shifts, transforming the forest around it.

What is fire? Fire is light and flame and heat.

It requires something to ignite,
oxygen—like an inhale—and a spark.
It has both the power to destroy
and the power to create.

Fire is a cosmic connection to the sun, that blaze in the sky. A reminder of stars and galaxies, of energy and elements radiating through space.

Our planet burns, too. The oldest known
wildfire smoldered 420 million years ago.
That's right. Fire on Earth has a birthday.

After that first fire, the world slowly changed. At first, it became drier. Ferns dwindled as new plants came into being—trees with thick bark and flowering shrubs filling the spaces opened by flames.

More fires burned.

Animals had to adapt, too.
By burrowing, diving, fleeing the heat.
By eating the new plants.

The world kept changing—
drying and cooling,
wetting and heating—
and fires kept burning.
Life as we know it evolved with fire.

For people long ago, fire meant more than survival. It was ritual, bonding them together. Sharing stories. Tending a flame.

Tending a flame to care for the land.

Now fire is this:
A wailing siren.
A home charred to the frame.
A town uniting.

Fire is also this:
An opening pine cone.
A seed released onto warm ash.
A fireweed sprouting.

A beetle, drawn by smoke and heat,
deposits eggs inside blaze-softened trees.
A woodpecker, also drawn by smoke and heat,
arrives soon after to eat larvae that emerge.

It is a campfire, now cool and damp,

and a wildland fire carefully tended.

As fires around the world come and go,
people will continue living with them.

By understanding fires past
and fires present. By adapting.

For fire is as essential as sunlight and rain. As fundamental to our life as the air we breathe.

Somewhere on Earth,
a fire smolders.

Witness its smoke
and glow
and power.

Fire shaped our world.
Together, we will change the future.

Author's Note

Gather around a campfire. Wood is stacked log cabin–style, with paper or tinder in its center. Surrounding this structure is air, which contains the element oxygen. A match is struck. Combine the right amount of both fuel and oxygen with a spark, either human-made or from a bolt of lightning, and fire comes to life.

For most of Earth's history, fires could not burn. Around 443 million years ago, the first vascular plants—plants with a special system to move water through their cells—evolved on land and flourished. Plants give off oxygen, and more plants meant both more oxygen and more fuels. When oxygen levels and available fuels on Earth increased, fire was born. The first fossil evidence of fire is the 420-million-year-old charcoal remains of a plant found in England.

Natural landscape fires were part of the world that humans evolved in. Fossil fire pits found in Africa suggest that early human ancestors started using fire on purpose between 1.6 million and 800,000 years ago. Most scientists agree that regular fire use changed human lives in two ways. First, humans began eating cooked food, which is easier to chew. They no longer required large jaws to eat a meal, so humans developed the smaller jaws we have today. Cooked food also offers more energy, and some scientists think this allowed early humans to grow bigger brains. Second, fires provided warmth and protection. As humans started spending time around fires, they had more opportunities to communicate and work together. Using fires in this way likely helped people develop language and expand their groups.

Humans are the only animal species that uses fire purposefully. Indigenous groups in the Americas, Aboriginal people in Australia, and farming communities in Europe use fire in complex ways and have done so for thousands of years. Traditional burning practices rely on knowledge of where to burn, what time of year or under what conditions to burn, and how to ignite and manage a fire for a specific purpose. For example, in the fall, Indigenous people across the western U.S. set fire to overgrown willow patches to reduce the old, dead wood and encourage new shoots that are strong and straight and prized for making baskets. These cultural fire-management practices determine which plants survive and ultimately shape the ecosystems we have today.

Landscape fire is a necessary component of many healthy ecosystems. Most ecosystems dependent on fire, such as prairies and coniferous forests, burn in a kind of pattern; some areas may burn every ten years or so. Frequent, low, or moderate fires return plant nutrients to the soil and help fire-dependent plants such as wire grass to flower. They also remove the top layer of decomposing plant material on a forest floor (called litter), making a better growing environment for seeds.

Some forests are adapted to more intense

landscape fires. The heat produced by such fires can cause dormant seeds to crack open and sprout. It also allows certain trees to release their seeds. One famous example of this process, known as serotiny, is the giant sequoia. Animals also benefit from fire, including bats that hunt in forests opened up by fire and roost in burned tree trunks.

Destructive fires, often called wildfires, have become more common. In ecosystems where they are expected, fires are more intense and often burn more land. Fires are also appearing in unexpected places, such as the Arctic. This increased frequency stems from both a shift in perspectives about fire as well as the effects of human-caused climate change. Around two hundred years ago, a new idea emerged that fire was purely destructive. Many countries started preventing and putting out fires, hoping to protect forests and people. But over time, eliminating traditional approaches to fire management actually has had the opposite effect. Putting out or suppressing fires has left more trees and plants as fuels, leading to larger, catastrophic wildfires.

Climate change has also affected the kinds of fires we see today, such as the wildfires in Australia and western North America in recent years. A warming climate often means longer periods of drought or times when there is less rainfall. This results in drier forests, which increases the risk of larger, more dangerous wildfires. Higher springtime temperatures can have a surprisingly similar result. More plant growth provides additional fuels for summer fires that are hotter and longer.

Climate change not only affects plant communities in ways that impact fires, but animal communities as well. Around the world, various kinds of bark beetles have multiplied in warmer temperatures and drier conditions. Beetle larvae can survive mild winters, and adults can reproduce faster and more often. By living in and feeding on drought-weakened trees, increased beetle populations threaten entire forests, leaving stands of dead trees now vulnerable to wildfires. An increase in wildfires across the globe threatens biodiversity of both plants and animals.

Fortunately, there is a lot that can be done to protect ecosystems and prevent dangerous wildfires. Indigenous groups are sharing their knowledge with government organizations. More and more foresters and fire managers are using planned fires (called prescribed burns) to reduce the amount of plant material available to burn out of control in the future. Fires in remote areas can be allowed to burn naturally. Firefighters use science to support healthy burns and also to suppress fires when deemed necessary.

With more wildfires expected in the future, it's important for decision makers to consider how we manage fire, and also how we live with it. We can construct fire-resistant houses and choose to build in areas where wildfires are less common. We can widen roads to allow safe passage of cars and fire engines and to act as a barrier to spreading wildfires. We can accept that co-existing with fire means adapting to new living conditions, such as more smoke in our skies. We can be curious and learn more about why fire is necessary in many environments. And we can educate others.

As you watch the campfire flicker, think of how fire changed life on Earth and how people are continuing to change with it. And when all that's left in the fire ring is glowing embers, be responsible and put the fire out!

Further Reading

Furgang, Kathy. *Wildfires.* Washington, DC: National Geographic Kids, 2015.

Peluso, Beth A. *The Charcoal Forest: How Fire Helps Animals and Plants.* Missoula, MT: Mountain Press Publishing Company, 2007.

Simon, Seymour. *Wildfires.* New York: HarperCollins, 2016.

Thiessen, Mark. *Extreme Wildfire.* Washington, DC: National Geographic Kids, 2016.

Wolff, Ashley. *Wildfire.* New York: Beach Lane Books, 2021.

Websites

www.ready.gov/kids/disaster-facts/wildfires
www.nps.gov/subjects/fire/fire-basics-for-kids.htm
www.SmokeyBear.com/en/smokey-for-kids
www.ReadyForWildfire.org
www.BrigadeKids.com.au

For Dad, in spite of everything, and for Karsten, whose heart burns so brightly. —J. C.

Text copyright © 2023 by Joanna Cooke
Illustrations copyright © 2023 by Cornelia Li and Diāna Renžina

YOSEMITE
CONSERVANCY
yosemite.org

Yosemite Conservancy inspires people to support projects and programs that preserve Yosemite and enrich the visitor experience.

Library of Congress Cataloging-in-Publication Data

Names: Cooke, Joanna, 1975- author. | Li, Cornelia, illustrator.
Title: Fire shapes the world / Joanna Cooke ; illustrated by Cornelia Li.
Description: Yosemite National Park : Yosemite Conservancy, 2023 | Audience: Grades 2-3 | Summary: "This nonfiction picture book presents Earth's long history with fire, and how humans, plants, and animals have adapted to this element as an integral part of their existence"--
   Provided by publisher.
Identifiers: LCCN 2021029502 (print) | LCCN 2021029503 (ebook) | ISBN 9781951179137 (hardcover) | ISBN 9781951179212 (epub)
Subjects: LCSH: Fire--History--Juvenile literature. | Fire--Social aspects--Juvenile literature. | Fire ecology--Juvenile literature. | Wildfires--Juvenile literature.
Classification: LCC GN417 .C66 2022 (print) | LCC GN417 (ebook) | DDC 363.37--dc23
LC record available at https://lccn.loc.gov/2021029502
LC ebook record available at https://lccn.loc.gov/2021029503

Design by Indya McGuffin

Printed in China

1 2 3 4 5 6 – 27 26 25 24 23